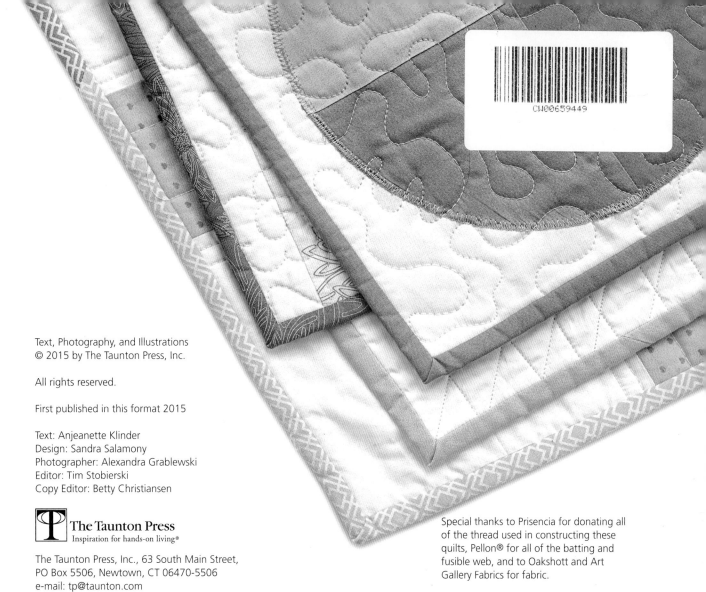

Text, Photography, and Illustrations
© 2015 by The Taunton Press, Inc.

First published in this format 2015

Text: Anjeanette Klinder
Design: Sandra Salamony
Photographer: Alexandra Grablewski
Editor: Tim Stobierski
Copy Editor: Betty Christiansen

T The Taunton Press
Inspiration for hands-on living®

The Taunton Press, Inc., 63 South Main Street,
PO Box 5506, Newtown, CT 06470-5506
e-mail: tp@taunton.com

Threads® is a trademark of The Taunton Press, Inc.,
registered in the U.S. Patent and Trademark Office.

The following names/manufacturers appearing in
Baby Quilts are trademarks: FriXion®, Lincoln Logs®,
Pellon®, Shout®.

Library of Congress Cataloging-in-Publication Data

Klinder, Anjeanette, author.
  Baby quilts : simple, colorful designs for little ones /
Anjeanette Klinder.
    pages cm
  ISBN 978-1-63186-401-8
  1. Children's quilts. 2. Patchwork--Patterns. 3.
Quilting--Patterns. I. Title.
  TT835.K554 2016
  746.46--dc23
                              2015036545

Printed in the United States of America
10 9 8 7 6 5 4 3 2 1

Special thanks to Prisencia for donating all
of the thread used in constructing these
quilts, Pellon® for all of the batting and
fusible web, and to Oakshott and Art
Gallery Fabrics for fabric.

Contents

QUILTING TECHNIQUES

FABRIC TIPS

There are two kinds of quilters: those who prewash their fabrics and those who do not. Either option is okay. If you are afraid of fabric bleeding, as hand-dyed or batik fabric can, you may want to prewash. I suggest you use quilting cotton and always follow the manufacturer's instructions for washing fabrics (they are listed on the end of all bolts of fabric). Whatever you decide to do, I suggest either washing all quilt top fabric or not washing any quilt top fabric so that all of the fabric in the quilt will act the same way; washing some fabrics and not others can lead to shrinkage or faded colors in some spots but not others. It is better for the entire quilt to be cohesive. I don't prewash my fabric, in most cases. When I wash the finished quilt, I wash it with a few color-catching sheets (such as those made by Shout®) to catch anything that happens to bleed.

ESSENTIAL QUILTING TOOLS

Sewing machine
The most important feature in a sewing machine used for quilting is the ability to sew a straight stitch. I also like to quilt with free-motion movement, which means I need to be able to cover or drop the feed dogs.

Needles
A universal needle works well for all of these quilts. I change the needle with every quilt to ensure accuracy and keep the machine from skipping stitches.

Rotary cutter
This great tool makes cutting fabric a breeze. Take care not to cut yourself with it, and always close the cutter when you are done cutting.

Self-healing cutting mat
Used with a rotary cutter, this makes cutting your fabrics to size and shape much easier.

See-through printed grid ruler
I suggest a ruler that has a 45-degree angle marked on it, which is useful for a few quilts in this booklet. Other helpful rulers include a large square to square up your corners after quilting and a long ruler to cut width-of-fabric cuts.

Seam ripper
This makes ripping seams to correct mistakes a breeze.

Specialty sewing feet
A walking foot is your best friend when sewing straight-line stitches, stitching in the ditch, and stitching on your binding. A free-motion or darning foot is also a great feature when you want to add a little detail and free-form movement to your quilting. I would suggest a free-motion foot only if you are able to cover or drop the feed dogs.

Pins
I suggest a nice thin pin. When I pin, I start at the outside edges. Every seam intersection and any length over about 5 in. gets a pin.

Iron and ironing board
You don't need to go crazy on an iron, but it should be heavy and have steam options. An ironing board should be sturdy to prevent accidents.

PINNING AND STARCHING

I pin every seam before I sew it. Lay the two pieces RST (right sides together), lining up the right raw edges together and matching the length of each piece. Pin the pieces together and pull the pins out before they reach the presser foot. You do not want to sew over a pin. I like to starch all my fabric before cutting. The starch will shrink or size the fabric a little. Also, it makes the fabric stiff and easier to work with. If I am working with any bias seams or edges, or tricky fabrics, I sometimes starch several times to make the whole quilt-making process easier.

HOW TO CONSTRUCT A QUILT SANDWICH

1. Working on a large, flat surface at least the size of your quilt backing, lay the backing fabric right side down. Make sure the backing fabric is perfectly smooth and flat; you can use several pieces of painter's tape to secure the fabric to the work surface if you'd like. Apply spray baste adhesive.

2. Place your batting on top of the backing. Smooth the batting until it is perfectly flat; you don't want the finished quilt to have bunched-up batting.

3. Lay the quilt top right side up on top of the batting. Smooth the quilt top to ensure there are no bunches

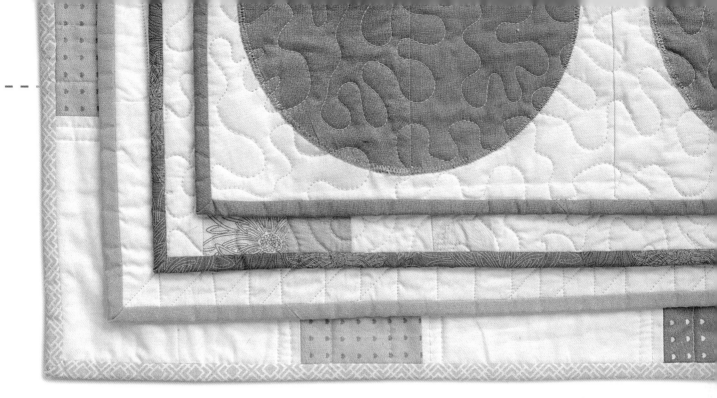

or bubbles. Roll half of the quilt top back toward the center of the quilt. You should have 2 in. of batting peeking out from underneath the quilt top, and 2 in. of backing fabric peeking out from under the batting. Apply spray baste to the batting and carefully roll the top onto the batting. Repeat with the other half of the quilt top.

QUILTING THE QUILT

Once the quilt sandwich is constructed and basted, you can move on to quilting the quilt. You can hand- or machine-quilt, depending on your preference and experience. I quilted all of the quilts in this booklet on a machine. A number of the quilts are quilted with straight-line stitches, which are much easier for a beginner, but the others are done in a free-motion style.

BINDING YOUR QUILT

1. For these quilts, I used continuous-length, double-fold, straight-of-grain binding in a 2½-in. width. When preparing to bind your quilt, sew any binding strips together end to end and press lengthwise with wrong sides together to create a single, long binding strip. I join the strips at a 45-degree angle, but sewing a straight line is fine too. Press the binding WST (wrong sides together) down the length. Prepare your quilt sandwich by trimming all the edges of the batting and backing. Use a large square ruler in each corner to make sure your quilt is square.

2. Starting about 6 in. to 8 in. from the first corner, place the binding on the quilt top, raw edges aligned, and pin one side in place. The folded edge should be toward the quilt. Using a walking foot if possible, leave a tail of 6 in. to 8 in. from the start of the binding and begin stitching a ¼-in. seam allowance. Stop when you are ¼ in. from the first corner. Remove the quilt from the machine and fold the binding up at a 45-degree angle. Fold the binding back straight down, keeping the raw edge lined up with the raw edge on the new side of the quilt. There will be a triangular tuck left. Pin the binding to this new side of the quilt.

3. Starting at the edge of the quilt, stitch down the length of the next side until you reach the next corner, then repeat the process in Step 2. When you get to the last side, leave a tail of 6 in. to 8 in. again. Leave a few inches to overlap the beginning layer of the binding, and trim off any excess.

4. You need to trim any excess binding fabric before joining your ends. Place the two ends together along your quilt edge and find where they meet. Add ¼ in. to each end, at this point. Remove excess fabric and sew the two ends together with a ¼-in. seam to complete the continuous loop of binding. Finger-press the seam and continue stitching the remaining binding to the quilt.

5. Press the binding flat. Wrap the folded edge of the binding around to the backside of the quilt. Pin the binding around the edge of the quilt. From the top of the quilt, sew the binding down by machine-stitching in the ditch on the front, or by hand-stitching on the back-side. When you reach each corner, take care to create a miter. If you are using a machine, stop right in the corner with the needle down and pivot, then continue sewing the next side.

FLY HOME FLYING GEESE QUILT

Flying geese are a favorite of quilters and kiddies everywhere. To the former, they are versatile units that can be used in many ways. To the latter, they are cute birds with honking voices who love to gobble up day-old bread. Why not combine the two? Soft blues in ascending hues add dimension and movement to this quilt, while calming your little one for his nap.

YOU'LL NEED

Note: All fabrics are 42 in. wide.

¼ yd. each of 5 different blue fabrics in ascending hues

1¼ yd. white fabric for background

½ yd. off-white or light patterned fabric for Flying Geese background

½ yd. fabric for binding

1⅛ yd. fabric of your choice for backing

Batting for 40-in. by 40-in. quilt

Rotary cutter

Self-healing cutting mat

Ruler with a 45-degree angle clearly marked

Marking pen (I use a water-soluble or erasable pen such as FriXion®)

Thread

Pins

Scissors

Iron

Sewing machine

Optional free-motion foot for quilting

Optional walking foot for quilting and applying binding

EXPERIENCE LEVEL

Intermediate

FINISHED SIZE

40-in. by 40-in. finished quilt

10-in. by 10-in. finished blocks

CUTTING INSTRUCTIONS

For binding, cut:
5 strips measuring 2½ in. by the width of the fabric of at least 42 in., selvages cut off.

From each of the 5 blue fabrics, cut:
Note: Because you will work with the bias edge when constructing the Flying Geese units, be sure to starch the blue fabric before cutting.

1 rectangle measuring 4½ in. by the width of the fabric of at least 42 in., selvages cut off. Cut each of these into 10 strips measuring 4½ in. by 2½ in.

From white fabric, cut:
4 rectangles measuring 10½ in. by the width of the fabric of at least 42 in., selvages cut off. Cut 2 of these rectangles into six 10½-in. by 10½-in. squares each. Cut 1 of the remaining rectangles into ten 10½-in. by 2½-in. strips. Cut the final rectangle into ten 10½-in. by 4½-in. strips.

From the fabric to be used as background for Flying Geese, cut:
Note: Because you will work with the bias edge when constructing the Flying Geese units, be sure to starch the Flying Geese background fabric before cutting.

7 strips measuring 2½ in. by the width of the fabric of at least 42 in., selvages cut off. Cut these strips into a total of one hundred 2½-in. by 2½-in. squares.

1. Assemble the Flying Geese units. Start by marking a diagonal line on the wrong side of all one hundred 2½-in. by 2½-in. background squares. The line should go from corner to corner. With right sides together (RST), place the marked background square on top of a blue 4½-in. by 2½-in. strip. The marked line on the background square should be going from one top corner of the blue strip to the center bottom of the blue strip. Pin. Using a straight stitch, sew directly on the marked line.

Cut off both the blue and the background fabric that is below the stitched line, maintaining a ¼-in. seam allowance **(Figure 1)**. Fold the background fabric down, so that the right side is showing, and press in the direction of the background fabric. Repeat this process on the other side of the blue strip, with a second marked background fabric square, so that you finish with a Flying Geese unit **(Figure 2)**. Construct a total of 50 Flying Geese units. You should have 10 units in each shade of blue.

2. Assemble the Flying Geese Blocks. Organize the Flying Geese units into columns of 5 units each. Each column should have hues organized in ascending order from lightest to darkest. Pin. Using a straight stitch and maintaining a ¼-in. seam allowance, sew units together to form a column, taking care not to sew through any of the points. Referring to **Figure 3**, using a straight stitch, and maintaining a ¼-in. seam allowance, sew 1 precut 10½-in. by 4½-in. strip of white fabric to the left side of the Flying Geese column. Then, sew 1 precut 10½-in. by 2½-in. strip of white fabric to the right side of the column. Repeat this process to create 10 total Flying Geese Blocks. Trim each block to 10½ in. by 10½ in.

3. Assemble the quilt top. Referring to Figure 4, lay out the blocks in 4 horizontal rows. Pin. Using a straight stitch and maintaining a ¼-in. seam allowance, sew each row of blocks together. Press the seams of each column in one direction, alternating directions with each row. Maintaining a ¼-in. seam allowance, join the rows together to complete the quilt top. Press seams in one direction.

4. Construct and bind the quilt. Following the instructions on p. 2, construct a quilt sandwich by layering the quilt top, batting, and backing fabric. Baste the 3 layers in place. Once you have finished basting, you can quilt as desired. I quilted a free-motion meandering loop pattern reminiscent of a bird's feathers (fitting for this quilt!), taking care not to quilt on top of the Flying

Geese columns. Doing this gave the quilt some depth by allowing the beautiful Flying Geese, which I outlined in running stitch, to pop.

Following the instructions on p. 3, bind the quilt. I used a variety of the fabrics for the Flying Geese blocks to tie everything together, but you can use whatever fabric you like.

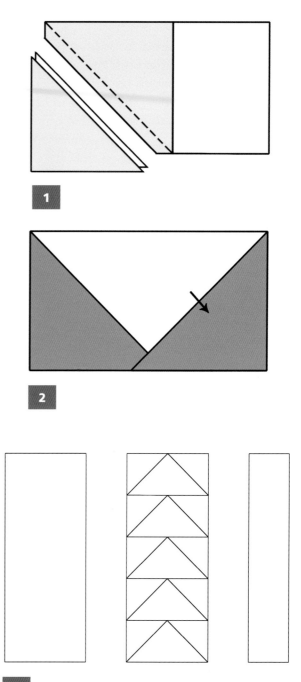

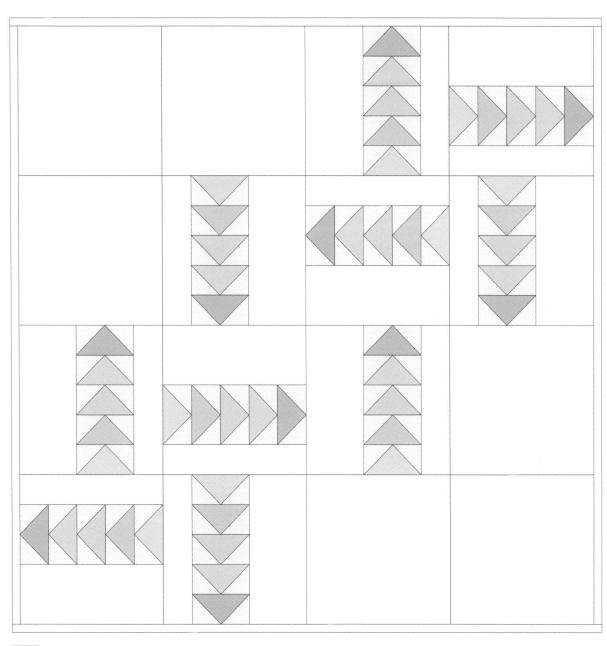

T I P I chose five different hues of blue for my quilt to achieve a calming effect, but you can use five hues of any color family you choose. Hues of green would also look especially nice and keep the calming feeling. Hues of orange or yellow would bring a bit more energy to the quilt.

TWO SCOOPS CIRCLE APPLIQUÉ QUILT

This easy appliqué quilt in sherbet colors captures the fun of summer. The simple construction is perfect for you to practice your quilting skills. Just make sure you have some sherbet on hand to reward yourself when you're done!

YOU'LL NEED

Note: All fabrics are 42 in. wide.

1¼ yd. white fabric for background

¼ yd. Fabric A (as shown, pink)

¼ yd. Fabric B (as shown, yellow)

¼ yd. Fabric C (as shown, purple)

⅛ yd. Fabric D (as shown, peach)

⅛ yd. Fabric E (as shown, green)

⅛ yd. Fabric F (as shown, blue)

½ yd. fabric of your choice for binding

1⅛ yd. fabric of your choice for backing

Batting for 30-in. by 40-in. quilt

Lightweight paper-backed fusible web

Rotary cutter

Self-healing cutting mat

Ruler

Thread

Pins

Scissors

Iron

Sewing machine

Optional free-motion foot for quilting

Optional walking foot for applying binding

EXPERIENCE LEVEL

Beginner

FINISHED SIZE

30-in. by 40-in. finished quilt

10-in. by 10-in. finished blocks

CUTTING INSTRUCTIONS

For binding, cut:
4 strips measuring 4½ in. by the width of the fabric of at least 42 in., selvages cut off.

From Fabric A (as shown, pink), cut:
2 rectangles measuring 4½ in. by the width of the fabric of at least 42 in., selvages cut off. Cut this into eleven 4½-in. by 4½-in. squares.

From Fabric B (as shown, yellow) and Fabric C (as shown, purple), cut:
2 rectangles from each measuring 4½ in. by the width of the fabric of at least 42 in., selvages cut off. Cut each of these into ten 4½-in. by 4½-in. squares.

From Fabric D (as shown, peach), cut:
1 rectangle measuring 4½ in. by the width of the fabric of at least 42 in., selvages cut off. Cut this into seven 4½-in. by 4½-in. squares.

From Fabric E (as shown, green) and Fabric F (as shown, blue), cut:
1 rectangle from each measuring 4½ in. by the width of the fabric of at least 42 in., selvages cut off. Cut each of these into five 4½-in. by 4½-in. squares.

Note: You will have a total of forty-eight 4½-in. squares of colored fabric.

From white fabric, cut:
2 rectangles measuring 10½ in. by the width of the fabric of at least 42 in., selvages cut off. Cut each of these into six 10½-in. squares.

Note: You will have twelve 10½-in. squares of white fabric.

From lightweight paper-backed fusible web, cut:
twelve 10½-in. squares.

1. Assemble the Four-Patch. Select 4 of the 4½-in. squares in an assortment of colors (it may be helpful for you to plan out your colorway in advance to know how your quilt will look before you begin sewing). With right sides together (RST), pin and sew 2 of the squares together using a straight stitch and maintaining a ¼-in. seam allowance. Repeat this process with the 2 remaining squares **(Figure 1)**. Using a straight stitch and maintaining a ¼-in. seam allowance, join the 2 pairs together. Be sure to match the center seams. The unit will measure 8 in. Repeat this process to make a total of 12 Four-Patch units.

Following the manufacturer's instructions, fuse 1 of the precut sheets of lightweight fusible web to the back of each Four-Patch unit. Once the web has been applied, cut an 8-in. circle from each Four-Patch unit. The spot where the 4 patches come together should lie in the center of the circle **(Figure 2)**.

2. Prepare for appliqué. Fold each white 10½-in. square in half both vertically and horizontally, and finger-press lightly to make a placement guide for the appli-qué. Following the manufacturer's instructions, fuse the Four-Patch circle onto the white square, matching the seams to the placement guides **(Figure 3)**. Repeat this process to make a total of 12 appliqué blocks. Using a matching thread, stitch around the border of each circle to finish the appliqué. I used a zigzag stitch, but you could also use a blanket stitch or appliqué stitch.

3. Assemble the quilt top. Referring to **Figure 4**, arrange the finished blocks into 4 horizontal rows. Be sure you are happy with the block and color placement before you begin sewing. Pin. Using a straight stitch and maintaining a ¼-in. seam allowance, sew each row of blocks together. Press the seams in one direc-tion, alternating direction with each row. Sew the rows together with a straight stitch and maintaining a ¼-in. seam allowance to complete the quilt top. Press any remaining seams in one direction.

4. Construct and bind the quilt. Following the instructions on p. 2, construct a quilt sandwich by layer-ing the quilt top, batting, and backing fabric. Baste the 3 layers in place. Once you have finished basting, you can quilt as desired. I quilted a free-motion meandering pattern to help blend the elements together.

Following the instructions on p. 3, bind the quilt. I used ½ yd. of the peach fabric (Fabric D) for my binding in order to tie my quilt together visually. You can use any fabric you want, but I recommend sticking with one of the fabrics that you used in constructing your quilt top.

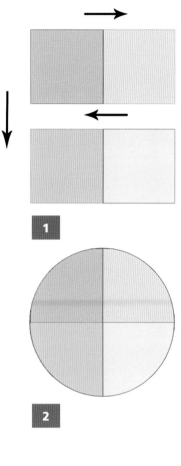

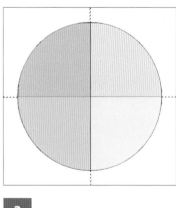

T I P

Are you more of an ice cream fan? Change up the pattern by using varying shades of brown and off-white to achieve a chocolate-vanilla swirl effect!

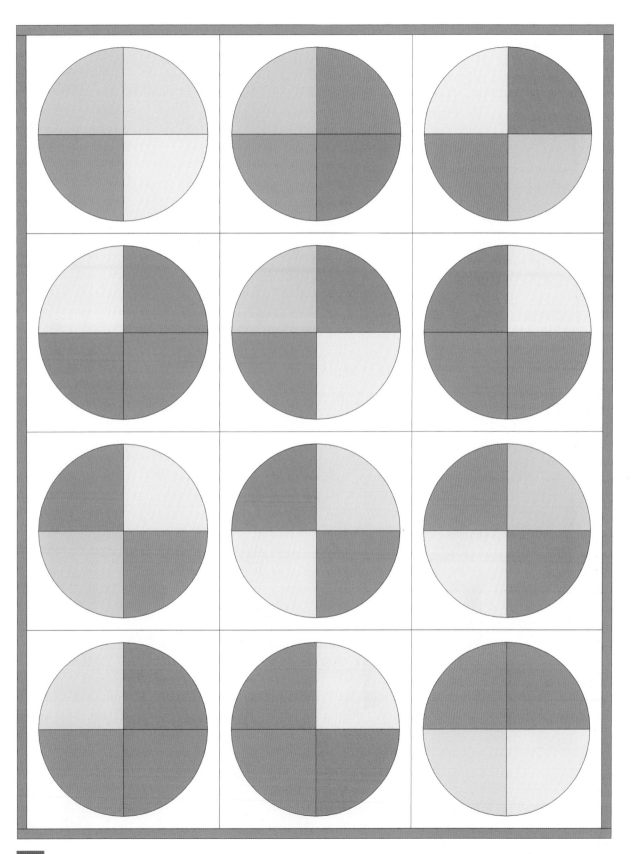

LINCOLN LOG CABIN QUILT

The strips of fabric used to construct the blocks of this simple log cabin quilt are reminiscent of another favorite childhood toy—Lincoln Logs®! The fabric is all straight cut, which means there aren't any bias edges to worry about. This is a perfect quilt for beginners, and its small size makes it ideal for covering a baby in a stroller.

YOU'LL NEED

Note: All fabrics are 42 in. wide.

⅛ yd. Fabric A (as shown, dark pink)
⅛ yd. Fabric B (as shown, peach)
½ yd. Fabric C (as shown, light pink)
½ yd. Fabric D (as shown, light peach)
⅓ yd. Fabric E (as shown, white)
⅓ yd. fabric of your choice for binding
1 yd. fabric of your choice for backing
Batting for 34-in. by 34-in. quilt
Rotary cutter
Self-healing cutting mat
Ruler
Thread
Pins
Scissors
Iron
Sewing machine
Optional free-motion foot for quilting
Optional walking foot for applying binding

EXPERIENCE LEVEL

Beginner

FINISHED SIZE

34-in. by 34-in. finished quilt
8½-in. by 8½-in. finished blocks

CUTTING INSTRUCTIONS

For binding, cut:
4 strips measuring 2½ in. by the width of the fabric of at least 42 in., selvages cut off.

From Fabric A (as shown, dark pink), cut:
1 strip measuring 2 in. by the width of the fabric of at least 42 in., selvages cut off.

From Fabric B (as show, peach), cut:
2 strips measuring 2 in. by the width of the fabric of at least 42 in., selvages cut off.

From Fabric C (as shown, light pink), cut:
3 strips measuring 4¼ in. by the width of the fabric of at least 42 in., selvages cut off.

From Fabric D (as shown, light peach), cut:
3 strips measuring 2½ in. by the width of the fabric of at least 42 in., selvages cut off, and 3 strips measuring 2 in. by the width of the fabric.

From Fabric E (as shown, white), cut:
3 strips measuring 2½ in. by the width of the fabric of at least 42 in., selvages cut off, and 3 strips measuring 1½ in. by the width of the fabric.

1. Assemble the Log Cabin block. To assemble the Log Cabin block, you'll first need to assemble 3 strips of fabric. For the center strip, pin, then using a straight stitch and maintaining a ¼-in. seam allowance, sew together 1 precut strip of Fabric B, 1 precut strip of Fabric A, a second precut strip of Fabric B, and 1 precut strip of Fabric C **(Figure 1)**. Cut this strip of combined fabric into sixteen 2-in. center row strips **(Figure 2)**.

For the left log strip, pin, then using a straight stitch and maintaining a ¼-in. seam allowance, sew together 1 precut 2½-in. strip of Fabric D and 1 precut 1½-in. strip of Fabric E. Cut this strip of combined fabric into sixteen 9-in. strips **(Figure 3)**.

For the right log strip, pin, then using a straight stitch and maintaining a ¼-in. seam allowance, sew together 1 precut 2-in. strip of Fabric D and 1 precut 2½-in. strip of Fabric E. As for the left log strip, cut this strip of combined fabric into sixteen 9-in. strips.

Using a straight stitch and maintaining a ¼-in. seam allowance, pin and sew together 1 left log strip, 1 center row strip, and 1 right log strip. Repeat this process to make 16 total Log Cabin blocks. Trim the blocks to 9 in. by 9 in.

2. Assemble the quilt top. Referring to **Figure 4**, lay out the blocks in 4 horizontal rows. Vary the block orientation to add interest to the quilt. Pin. Using a straight stitch and maintaining a ¼-in. seam allowance, sew each row of blocks together. Press the seams for each row in one direction, alternating direction with each row. Use a straight stitch and maintain a ¼-in. seam allowance to sew the rows together and finish the quilt top.

3. Construct and bind the quilt. Following the instructions on p. 2, construct a quilt sandwich by layering the quilt top, batting, and backing fabric. Baste the 3 layers in place. Once you have finished basting, you can quilt as desired. I quilted a meandering, floral-inspired stitch over the entire quilt.

Following the instructions on p. 3, bind the quilt. I used Fabric A (as shown, dark pink) to bind my quilt, but you can use whatever fabric you choose.

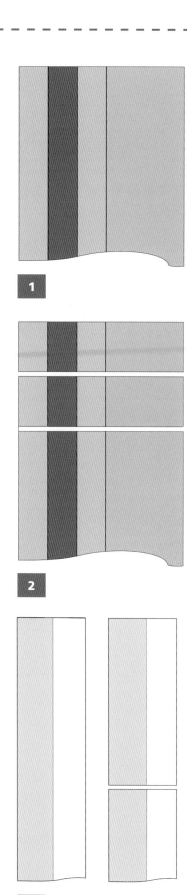

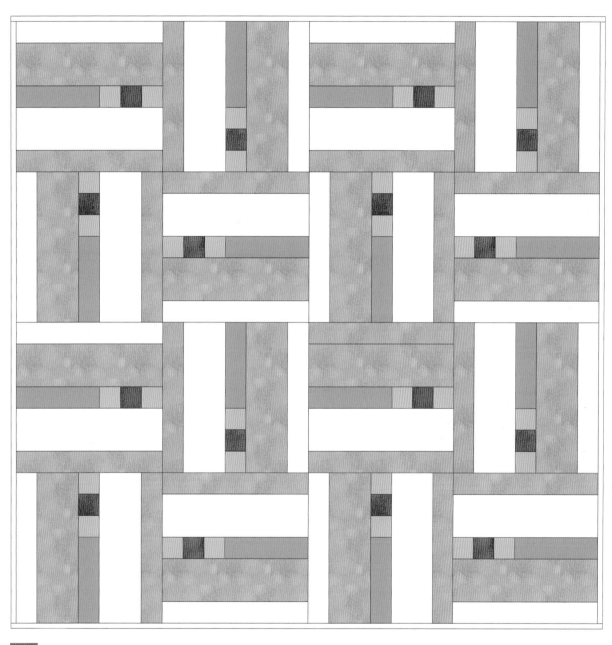

Log Cabin quilts typically have a red center to represent the hearth of the home. Think of different ways you can use the center as a bold accent, such as by using a bright print. Consider keeping the "logs" around the hearth warm or neutral.

LAZY SUNDAY IRISH CHAIN QUILT

What's better than a lazy Sunday spent with your little ones? A lazy Sunday cuddled up in a cozy, warm quilt! This project is simpler than you might think, and it's the perfect quilt to take on a Sunday picnic or stroll. I used shades of purple, but you can swap these out for any of your favorite colors.

YOU'LL NEED

Note: All fabrics are 42 in. wide.

½ yd. Fabric A (as shown, darkest purple)

⅔ yd. Fabric B (as shown, medium purple)

¼ yd. Fabric C (as shown, lightest purple)

1 yd. white fabric for background

½ yd. fabric of your choice for binding

1½ yd. fabric of your choice for backing

Batting for 40-in. by 50-in. finished quilt

Rotary cutter

Self-healing cutting mat

Ruler

Thread

Pins

Scissors

Iron

Sewing machine

Optional free-motion foot for quilting

Optional walking foot for applying binding

EXPERIENCE LEVEL
Intermediate

FINISHED SIZE
40-in. by 50-in. finished quilt
10-in. by 10-in. finished blocks

CUTTING INSTRUCTIONS

For binding, cut:
5 strips measuring 2½ in. by the width of the fabric of at least 42 in., selvages cut off.

From Fabric A (as shown, darkest purple), cut:
2 rectangles measuring 6½ in. by the width of the fabric of at least 42 in., selvages cut off.

From Fabric B (as shown, medium purple), cut:
3 strips measuring 2½ in. by the width of the fabric of at least 42 in., selvages cut off, and 3 strips measuring 4½ in. by the width of the fabric.

From Fabric C (as shown, lightest purple), cut:
3 strips measuring 2½ in. by the width of the fabric of at least 42 in., selvages cut off.

From white fabric, cut:
3 strips measuring 2½ in. by the width of the fabric of at least 42 in., selvages cut off, and 3 strips measuring 6½ in. by the width of the fabric. Cut the 6½-in. strips into twenty 6½-in. by 10½-in. rectangles.

These three shades of purple fabric brought to my mind a certain singing dinosaur. Does your little one have a favorite cartoon character? The next time you're watching television imagine how the character would look in three basic colors or hues.

1. Assemble Block 1. Using a straight stitch and maintaining a ¼-in. seam allowance, pin and sew 1 precut 4½-in. strip of Fabric B (as shown, medium purple) to each side of a precut 2½-in. strip of white fabric. Press the seams to the purple fabric. Cut this combined fabric strip into strips measuring 2½ in. **(Figure 1)**. Make twenty 2½-in. strips of combined fabric (now called Unit A).

Using a straight stitch and maintaining a ¼-in. seam allowance, pin and sew 1 precut 2½-in. strip of Fabric B (as shown, medium purple) to each side of a precut 2½-in. strip of white fabric. Press the seams to the purple fabric. Cut this combined fabric strip into strips measuring 2½ in. **(Figure 2)**. Repeat to make twenty 2½-in. strips of combined fabric (now called Unit B).

Using a straight stitch and maintaining a ¼-in. seam allowance, pin and sew 1 Unit B to each side of a 6½-in. by 6½-in. square of Fabric A (as shown, darkest purple). Press the seams to the purple fabric. On the remaining two sides, using a straight stitch and maintaining a ¼-in. seam allowance, sew 1 Unit A. Repeat this process to make 10 Block 1 blocks. Trim each Block 1 blocks to 10½ in. by 10½ in.

2. Assemble Block 2. Using a straight stitch and maintaining a ¼-in. seam allowance, pin and sew 1 precut ½-in. strip of Fabric C (as shown, lightest purple) to each side of a 6½-in. strip of white fabric. Press the seams toward the white side. Cut this combined fabric strip into strips measuring 2½ in. **(Figure 3)**. Make twenty 2½-in. strips of this combined fabric (now called Unit C).

Using a straight stitch and maintaining a ¼-in. seam allowance, pin and sew 1 Unit C to each of the long sides of a precut 6½-in. by 10½-in. rectangle of white fabric. Press seams toward the white side. Repeat this process to make 10 Block 2 blocks. Trim each block to measure 10½ in. by 10½ in.

3. Assemble the quilt top. Referring to **Figure 4**, lay out the blocks in 5 horizontal rows. You will alternate between Block 1 and Block 2. Using a straight stitch and maintaining a ¼-in. seam allowance, pin and sew each row of blocks together. Press the seams for each row in one direction, alternating direction with each row. Use a straight stitch and maintain a ¼-in. seam allowance to pin and sew the rows together and finish the quilt top.

4. Construct and bind the quilt. Following the instructions on p. 2, construct a quilt sandwich by layering the quilt top, batting, and backing fabric. Baste the 3 layers in place and quilt as desired. I quilted a free-motion meander in the white portions of my quilt while simply outlining each purple component with a straight stitch to give the quilt some dimension.

Following the instructions on p. 3, bind the quilt. I used Fabric B (as shown, medium purple) to bind my quilt, but you can use whatever fabric you choose.

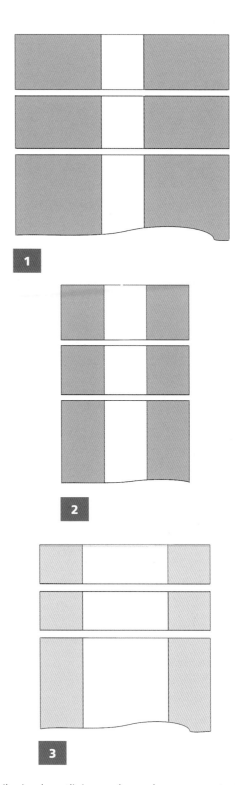

4

BUILDING BLOCKS QUILT

This easy quilt was inspired by a favorite toy of babies everywhere—building blocks! The quilt consists of four large blocks and uses six coordinating pattern fabrics in a scrappy way. Greens, blues, and grays make for a great boy-themed quilt, but try shades of pinks and reds if you have a little girl in mind.

YOU'LL NEED

Note: All fabrics are 42 in. wide.

½ yd. of 6 coordinating pattern fabrics

1 yd. white fabric for background

½ yd. fabric of your choice for binding

3 yd. fabric of your choice for backing

Batting for 48-in. by 48-in. quilt

Rotary cutter

Self-healing cutting mat

Ruler

Thread

Pins

Scissors

Iron

Sewing machine

Optional walking foot for quilting and applying binding

EXPERIENCE LEVEL

Beginner

FINISHED SIZE

48-in. by 48-in. finished quilt

24-in. by 24-in. finished blocks

CUTTING INSTRUCTIONS

For binding, cut:

5 strips measuring 2½ in. by the width of the fabric of at least 42 in., selvages cut off.

From pattern fabric, cut:

Two 3½-in. by 3½-in. squares and two 9½-in. by 3½-in. strips.

Note: Because of the scrappy nature of this pattern, you are going to need to repeat the pattern fabric cutting a total of 16 times, using any desired combination of your prints. The quilt I made uses 6 printed fabrics to create the pattern, with each fabric repeated a number of times to get the right fit.

From white fabric, cut:

1 strip measuring 6½ in. by the width of the fabric of at least 42 in., 4 strips measuring 6½ in. by the width of the fabric, and 1 strip measuring 3½ in. by the width of the fabric. From the first 6½-in. strip, cut four 6½-in. by 12½-in. strips, forty 6½-in. by 3½-in. strips, and sixteen 3½-in. by 3½-in. squares. From the remaining 6½-in. strips, cut forty-eight 6½-in. by 3½-in. strips. From the 3½-in. strip, cut twelve 3½-in. by 3½-in. squares.

1. Assemble the blocks. Referring to **Figure 1**, lay out the cut fabric into the block pattern to ensure that you have all of the pieces. Using a straight stitch and maintaining a ¼-in. seam allowance, pin and sew the block components together. Press the finished block. Repeat to form the 4 total blocks needed for the complete quilt.

2. Assemble the quilt top. Referring to **Figure 2**, lay the 4 blocks out on the work surface in 2 horizontal rows. Using a straight stitch and maintaining a ¼-in. seam allowance, pin and sew each set of 2 blocks together. Press the seams on the first row of quilt blocks in one direction; alternate the direction when pressing the seams of the second row of quilt blocks. Pin rows together, matching the seams at each intersection. Join the 2 rows to complete the quilt top, using a straight stitch and a ¼-in. seam allowance. Press the seams in one direction.

3. Construct and bind the quilt. Following the instructions on p. 2, construct a quilt sandwich by layering the quilt top, batting, and backing fabric. Baste the 3 layers in place. Once you have finished basting, you can quilt as desired. I quilted this quilt with a simple straight stitch, outlining the shapes of the "building block" portions of each quilt block in order to echo the design. Use a walking foot here if you have one. I quilted the inside border of the white squares and cross shapes with 2 lines of straight stitches and put an X in the center of each to add texture and interest to the finished piece.

Following the instructions on p. 3, bind the quilt. For my binding, I chose some of the extra green, blue, and gray fabric that I used to construct my quilt blocks. This helped to make the quilt as a whole feel cohesive. You can do this with your fabrics or bind the quilt with whatever fabric you choose.

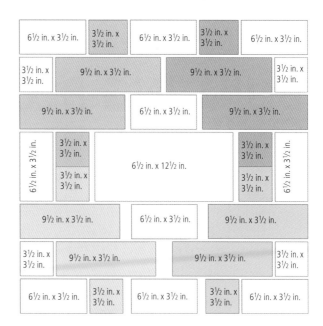

1

T I P This quilt is perfect for throwing down on the floor at playtime when the child is young, and it can then be used as a bed quilt once the child grows up. Or, reduce the size of the quilt easily by constructing, quilting, and binding a single block for a crib or two blocks for a toddler's bed. Simply adjust your fabric amounts accordingly.

2

RAINBOW DAYS QUILT

This stunning rainbow quilt was inspired by a scrappy, string quilt design that I tweaked for a more baby-friendly look. Because you will be working with the bias edge of fabric, make sure you starch your fabric before cutting to lessen distortion.

YOU'LL NEED

Note: All fabrics are 42 in. wide.

One 10-in. by 10-in. square each of 18 different fabrics

1½ yd. white fabric for background

½ yd. fabric of your choice for binding

1½ yd. fabric of your choice for backing

Batting for a 40-in. by 40-in. quilt

Rotary cutter

Self-healing cutting mat

Ruler with 45-degree angle clearly marked

Thread

Pins

Scissors

Iron

Sewing machine

Marking pen

Optional free-motion foot for quilting

Optional walking foot for applying binding

Optional rotating cutting mat (as there is a fair amount of trimming up)

EXPERIENCE LEVEL

Advanced

FINISHED SIZE

40-in. by 40-in. finished quilt

5-in. by 5-in. finished blocks

CUTTING INSTRUCTIONS

Note: Because you will be working with the bias edge, starch all fabrics before cutting.

For binding, cut:
5 strips measuring ½ in. by the width of the fabric of at least 42 in., selvages cut off.

From each 10-in. square of colored fabric, cut:
4 strips measuring 1½ in. by 8¼ in. and 4 strips measuring ¾ in. by 4 in. Finger-press all strips in half. Repeat for all 18 fabric squares.

From white fabric, cut:
4 strips measuring 6½ in. by the width of the fabric of at least 42 in., selvages cut off, 2 strips measuring 5½ in. by the width of the fabric, and 2 strips measuring 6¼ in. by the width of the fabric. Cut the 6½-in. strips into 72 strips measuring 2 in. by 6½ in. (finger-press in half). Cut the 5½-in. strips each into 40½-in. by 5½-in. strips (for the top and bottom of the quilt). Cut the 6¼-in. strips into twelve 6¼-in. by 6¼-in. squares; cut each in half diagonally to make 24 triangles, and finger-press each in half.

1. Assemble Unit 1. Work with the precut strips of a single color of fabric for each colored block. Referring to **Figure 1** and using a straight stitch and maintaining a ¼-in. seam allowance, pin and sew together one 1½-in. by 8¼-in. colored strip, one 2-in. by 6½-in. white strip, and one 1¾-in. by 4-in. colored strip. Be sure to match the center crease mark of each strip. This is Unit 1. Repeat this process to create a total of 4 Unit 1 units in each color, for a total of 72 Unit 1 units. For each of these groupings of 4 Unit 1 units, press as follows: Press the seams of 2 Unit 1 units toward the small colored rectangle and press the seams of the remaining 2 Unit 1 units toward the large rectangle. This will help the diamonds nestle later, when you complete the quilt top.

2. Assemble Block A. Lay out the 72 Unit 1 units as you wish the final quilt to appear. Those units that are on the outside will need to be sewn to a precut white half-square triangle. Choose an appropriate Unit 1 unit. Referring to **Figure 2,** lay 1 precut white half-square triangle of fabric on top of this Unit 1, right sides together (RST), and match the pressed creases. Using a straight stitch and maintaining a ¼-in. seam allowance, sew together and press. Lay a ruler on top of the block, lining up the diagonal seam with the 45-degree mark. Cut the block to measure 5½ in. by 5½ in. Repeat this process for all 24 outer Unit 1 units, resulting in 24 Block A blocks.

3. Assemble Block B. Referring to **Figure 3**, place a Unit 1 next to a second Unit 1 RST, and match their center creases. Pin. Using a straight stitch and maintaining a ¼-in. seam allowance, stitch the units together. This new block will consist of 2 differently colored Unit 1 units. Repeat for a total of 24 Block B blocks. As for Block A above, cut each block to measure 5½ in. by 5½ in.

4. Assemble the quilt top. Referring to **Figure 4**, lay out all of the blocks into 6 horizontal rows. Pin. Using a straight stitch and maintaining a ¼-in. seam allowance, sew each row together. Press seams in one direction; alternate direction for each row. Join the rows and press. Using a straight stitch and maintaining a ¼-in. seam allowance, pin and sew the precut 40½-in. by 5½-in. borders of white fabric to the top and bottom of the quilt.

5. Construct and bind the quilt. Following the instructions on p. 2, construct a quilt sandwich by layering the quilt top, batting, and backing fabric. Baste the

3 layers in place. Once you have finished basting, you can quilt as desired. With the help of a walking foot, I quilted around each component of my colored squares to echo the geometric pattern. I also quilted straight lines in the white border to make everything pop.

Following the instructions on p. 3, bind the quilt. I used some of the extra colored fabric that I had to bind my quilt, but you can use whatever fabric you choose.

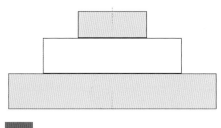

1

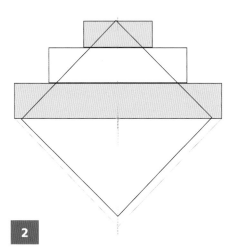

2

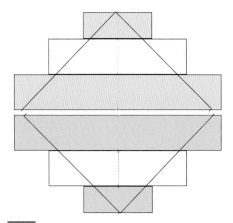

3

I made this fun quilt using a number of shades from each color family in order to give the quilt some movement and depth, but you can simplify things if you'd rather not buy this many types of fabric. Keep each row of rainbow blocks a single color, instead of different shades of that color, and you'll have a shorter fabric list.

WISH UPON A STAR QUILT

You'll always have a star to grant your wishes with this adorable quilt in soft pink fabric. The fabric is cut on the diagonal, which means you will be working with the bias, so make sure you starch your fabrics before you cut them out to stabilize everything.

YOU'LL NEED

Note: All fabrics are 42 in. wide.

½ yd. Fabric A (as shown, light solid pink)

½ yd. Fabric B (as shown, dark solid pink)

½ yd. Fabric C (as shown, light floral pink)

½ yd. Fabric D (as shown, dark floral pink)

1½ yd. white fabric for background

½ yd. fabric of your choice for binding

1½ yd. fabric of your choice for backing

Batting for 36-in. by 48-in. finished quilt

Rotary cutter

Self-healing cutting mat

Ruler

Thread

Pins

Scissors

Iron

Sewing machine

Marking pen

Optional free-motion foot for quilting

Optional walking foot for applying binding

Optional rotating cutting mat

EXPERIENCE LEVEL
Advanced

FINISHED SIZE
36-in. by 48-in. finished quilt

9-in. by 12-in. finished blocks

CUTTING INSTRUCTIONS

For binding, cut:
5 strips measuring 2½ in. by the width of the fabric of at least 42 in., selvages cut off.

From Fabrics C and D (as shown, light floral pink and dark floral pink) each, cut:
1 strip measuring 5 in. by the width of the fabric of at least 42 in., selvages cut off, 1 strip measuring 3½ in. by the width of the fabric, and 1 strip measuring 6½ in. by the width of the fabric. Cut the 5-in. strip into six 5-in. squares. Cut the ½-in. strip into twelve 3½-in. by 2-in. rectangles. Cut the 6½-in. strip into six 6½-in. by 3½-in. rectangles.

From Fabrics A and B (as shown, light solid pink and dark solid pink) each, cut:
1 strip measuring 5 in. by the width of the fabric of at least 42 in., selvages cut off, and 1 strip measuring 8¼ in. by the width of the fabric. Cut the 5-in. strip into six 5-in. by 5-in. squares. Cut the 8¼-in. strip into three 8¼-in. squares.

From white fabric, cut:
2 strips measuring 8¼ in. by the width of the fabric of at least 42 in., selvages cut off, 8 strips measuring 2 in. by the width of the fabric, and 2 strips measuring 6½ in. by the width of the fabric. Cut the 8¼-in. strips into six 8¼-in. by 8¼-in. squares. Cut 6 of the 2-in. strips into twenty-four 9½-in. by 2-in. rectangles. Cut the remaining 2-in. strips into two 36½-in. by 2-in. strips. Cut the 6½-in. strips into six 6½-in. by 9½-in. strips.

1. Make the half-square triangle (HST) units. Referring to **Figure 1** and working on the wrong side of an 8¼-in. by 8¼-in. square of white fabric, draw 2 diagonal lines from corner to corner, creating an X. Place this white fabric square on top of one 8¼-in. square of colored fabric, right sides together (RST). Pin. Sew a scant ¼-in. seam on each side of the drawn lines, through both squares of fabric, and press to set the seams. Using a rotary cutter and ruler, cut the square in half vertically and horizontally. Next, cut along the drawn lines so that you have 8 HST units. Press each unit open. Align the diagonal block with the 45-degree mark on the ruler and trim each HST unit to 3½ in. Repeat this process with all of the 8¼-in. squares of white and colored fabrics, for a total of 24 light solid pink/white HST units and 24 dark solid pink/white HST units. Repeat the above process with the 5-in. squares of fabric for a total of 48 light solid pink/light floral pink HST units and 48 dark solid pink/dark floral pink HST units. Trim each of these smaller HST units to measure 2 in.

2. Assemble the star blocks. Using a straight stitch and maintaining a ¼-in. seam allowance, pin and sew together two 2-in. HST units and press. Repeat for a total of 4 joined HST units for each block. Referring to **Figure 2**, arrange the block components into rows. Pin. Sew the components into rows, and then join the rows together and press to form a star unit. Sew a 9½-in. strip of white fabric onto both the right and left side of the star unit to finish the block, and press. Repeat this process until you have 6 light pink star blocks and 6 dark pink star blocks.

3. Assemble the quilt top. Referring to **Figure 3**, lay out the blocks in 5 horizontal rows. Rows 1, 3, and 5 will need a 9½-in. by 6½-in. rectangle of fabric on each side of the row to even it out. Using a straight stitch and maintaining a ¼-in. seam allowance, pin and sew the rows together. Press the seams of each row in one direction, alternating the direction with each row. Using a straight stitch and maintaining a ¼-in. seam allowance, sew the rows together. Sew one 36½-in. by 2-in. strip of white fabric to the top and bottom of the quilt top.

4. Construct and bind the quilt. Following the instructions on p. 2, construct a quilt sandwich by layering the quilt top, batting, and backing fabric. Baste the 3 layers in place then quilt as desired. I quilted a free-motion meander through the entire quilt.

Following the instructions on p. 3, bind the quilt. I used some of the extra colored fabric that I had to bind my quilt, but you can use whatever fabric you choose.

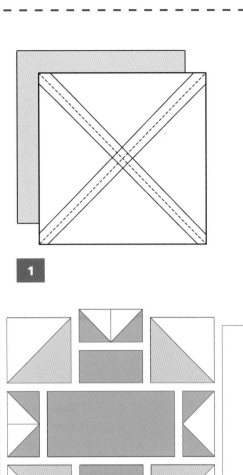

1

2

T I P

Star quilts are my favorite quilts to make. I use a rotating mat to make the half-square triangles (HST) because it makes trimming each HST unit to size fairly quick. If you're making this quilt for a boy, use yellows and whites for the stars and blue as the sky background for a soothing design.

3

Look for these other *Threads* Selects booklets at www.tauntonstore.com and wherever crafts are sold.

Small Projects to Quilt
Joan Ford

EAN: 9781627100977
8½ x 10⅞, 32 pages
Product# 078032
$9.95 U.S., $9.95 Can.

Prairie Girl Sewing
Jennifer Worick

EAN: 9781621139508
8½ x 10⅞, 32 pages
Product# 078029
$9.95 U.S., $9.95 Can.

Prairie Girl Gifts
Jennifer Worick

EAN: 9781621139492
8½ x 10⅞, 32 pages
Product # 078030
$9.95 U.S., $9.95 Can.

Easy-to-Sew Pillows

EAN: 9781621138266
8½ x 10⅞, 32 pages
Product# 078019
$9.95 U.S., $9.95 Can.

Easy-to-Sew Tote Bags

EAN: 9781621138297
8½ x 10⅞, 32 pages
Product# 078021
$9.95 U.S., $9.95 Can.

Easy-to-Sew Flowers

EAN: 9781621138259
8½ x 10⅞, 32 pages
Product# 078017
$9.95 U.S., $9.95 Can.

Easy-to-Sew Gifts

EAN: 9781621138310
8½ x 10⅞, 32 pages
Product # 078023
$9.95 U.S., $9.95 Can.

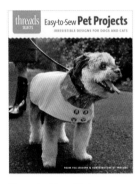

Easy-to-Sew Pet Projects

EAN: 9781621138273
8½ x 10⅞, 32 pages
Product# 078018
$9.95 U.S., $9.95 Can.

Easy-to-Sew Windows

EAN: 9781621138303
8½ x 10⅞, 32 pages
Product# 078022
$9.95 U.S., $9.95 Can.

Easy-to-Sew Handbags

EAN: 9781621138242
8½ x 10⅞, 32 pages
Product# 078016
$9.95 U.S., $9.95 Can.

Easy-to-Sew Kitchen

EAN: 9781621138327
8½ x 10⅞, 32 pages
Product# 078024
$9.95 U.S., $9.95 Can.

Easy-to-Sew Lace

EAN: 9781621138228
8½ x 10⅞, 32 pages
Product# 078014
$9.95 U.S., $9.95 Can.